Ocean
Life

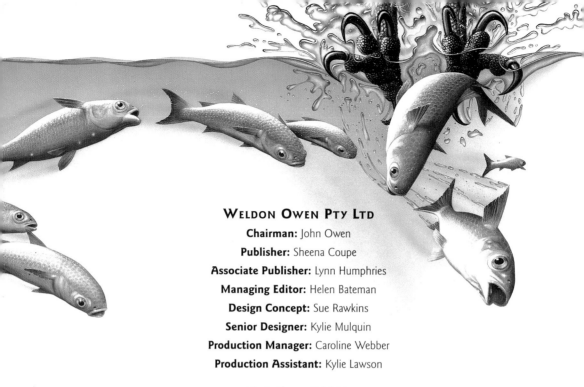

WELDON OWEN PTY LTD

Chairman: John Owen
Publisher: Sheena Coupe
Associate Publisher: Lynn Humphries
Managing Editor: Helen Bateman
Design Concept: Sue Rawkins
Senior Designer: Kylie Mulquin
Production Manager: Caroline Webber
Production Assistant: Kylie Lawson

Text: Sharon Dalgleish
Consultant: Craig Sowden, Curator, Sydney Aquarium
U.S. Editors: Laura Cavaluzzo and Rebecca McEwen

04 03 02 01 00 99
10 9 8 7 6 5 4 3 2 1

Published in the United States by
Shortland Publications, Inc.
P.O. Box 6195
Denver, CO 80206-0195

Printed in Australia.
ISBN: 0-7699-0480-7

CONTENTS

CURRENTS AND TIDES

The world's oceans are constantly moving. Huge bodies of water are pushed around the Earth in giant loops called currents. Ocean currents are caused by the wind and the spin of the Earth. North of the equator, currents flow to the right. South of the equator, they flow to the left. The level of the sea also rises and falls each day. These high and low tides are caused by the pull of the Moon and the Sun.

Clinging On

If you look underneath small animals in tidal zones, you'll see how they cling to rocks in the surf. Sea stars, or starfish, have hundreds of tiny suckers on their feet. Limpets and periwinkles have one big, muscular foot.

4

The Pull of the Moon

As the Moon orbits the Earth, the Moon's gravity pulls the oceans toward it. This causes a high tide.

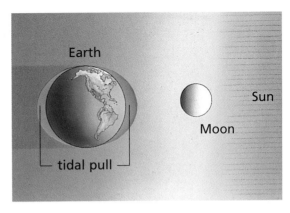

Earth

Sun

Moon

tidal pull

Ocean Litter

Litter dropped between South America and Antarctica might end up years later in Western Australia, New Zealand, southern Africa, the Seychelles, or Easter Island. Currents push ocean litter right around the world.

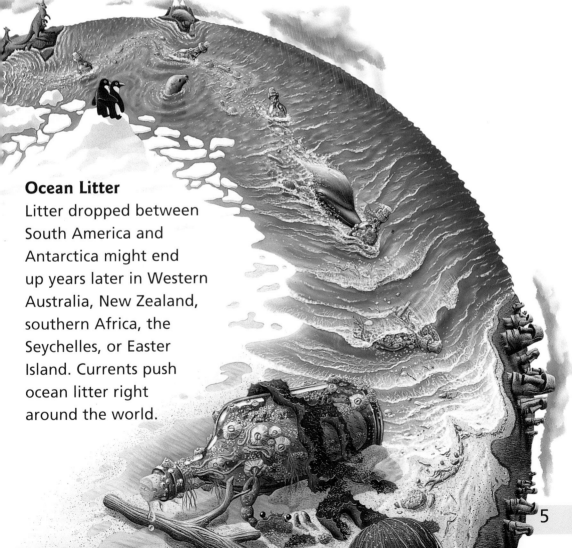

5

ON THE BOTTOM

Deep down on the ocean floor it is cold and dark. There's no light from the Sun, so no plants can grow. There are no waves. Everything is still. Cold water seeps down through cracks and is heated by lava. Hot water and black smoke gush out of chimneys into the icy stillness.

Deep-sea Dinosaurs
Primitive fish live on the seafloor. The eelpout feeds on tube worms.

Mussel-ing In
Mussels and giant clams filter tiny scraps of food from the water.

Underwater Volcanoes
Deep-sea creatures use the
sulphur from underwater
chimneys to make food.

Glow-in-the-dark Shark
The spined pygmy shark makes its
own light. Its skin glows in the dark.

Worm Garden
Tube worms live on bacteria that
they absorb through their skin.

MONSTERS

Early sailors braved unknown seas. At every port they told stories of huge monsters from the deep. Their maps were filled with drawings of weird sea creatures. One legend was of an octopus-like monster called a kraken that could sink a ship.

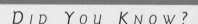

A Whale of a Monster

A story from the Bible tells how Jonah was swallowed by a whale. He lived in the whale's belly for three days before it spat him out again.

Breaking Up

The masts and rigging break up first. Then the upper deck collapses. Sediment builds up until the hull is completely filled.

after one year

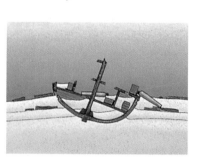

after ten years

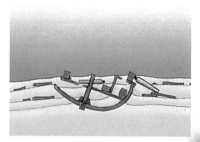

after fifty years

after eighty years

Precious Cargo

Sometimes pots and other finds are taken from a wreck. Special bags are filled with air to lift the treasure to the surface.

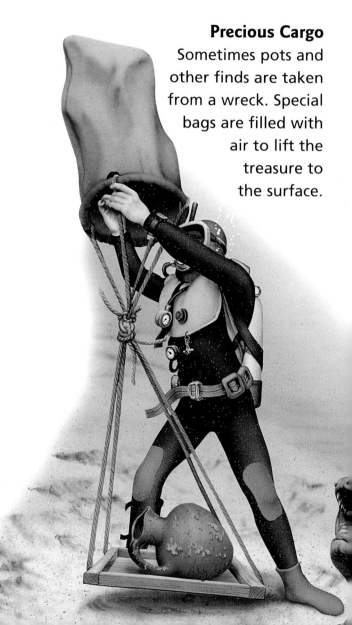

BURIED TREASURE

The ocean floor is littered with the wrecks of ancient and modern ships. Whatever the reason for a wreck—poor navigation, a raging storm, a fierce sea battle, or just bad luck—the ship's wreckage gives shelter to fish and other creatures of the sea. A sunken ship breaks up little by little through the years until it's filled with sediment.

Diving into the Past
Scuba divers can visit wrecks that are in shallow waters. Wrecks in deep water are much harder to find.

Underwater Air
Divers wear air tanks on their back so they can breathe under water.

Underwater Vacuum
A giant vacuum cleaner is used to suck up sediment.

Recording the Site
Archaeologists take a series of photographs to record every inch of a wreck site.

Site Grid
A grid on the seafloor helps archaeologists locate the exact position of objects.

Maritime archaeologists dive to the bottom of the ocean to explore shipwrecks. Wrecks from centuries ago are like sunken time capsules— they give us clues about how people lived in the past. Archaeologists try to leave a wreck exactly as they found it, so others can explore it and learn about the past.

Lights, Camera, Action!
When the water isn't too murky, maritime archaeologists can make video recordings of a site, using special underwater cameras.

13

Polar bears lie completely still on the ice beside a seal's breathing hole. When a seal pops up for air, the bear scoops it out with the claws on its front paws.

FOOD FROM THE SEA

The ocean provides food for many land animals. Grizzly bears catch salmon with the sharp claws on their front feet. Diving birds such as the osprey plunge from the sky to grab fish out of the water with their strong talons. People fish food from the sea using different types of nets, pots, baskets, and hooks.

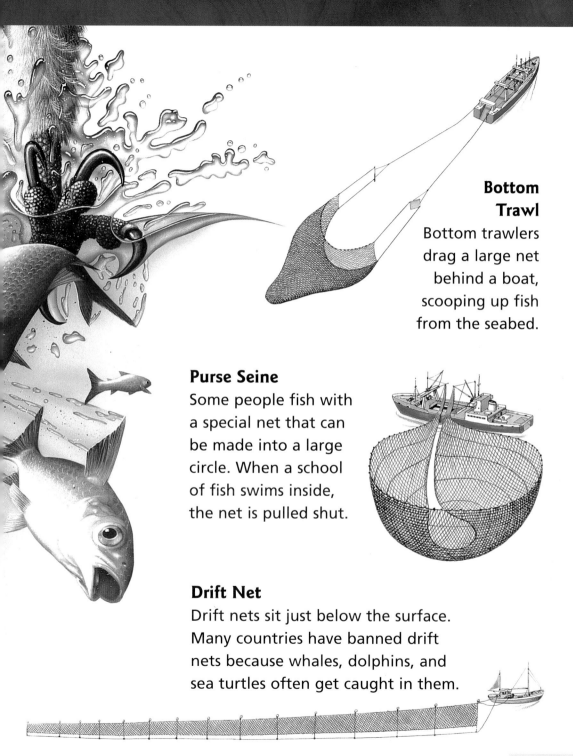

Bottom Trawl

Bottom trawlers drag a large net behind a boat, scooping up fish from the seabed.

Purse Seine

Some people fish with a special net that can be made into a large circle. When a school of fish swims inside, the net is pulled shut.

Drift Net

Drift nets sit just below the surface. Many countries have banned drift nets because whales, dolphins, and sea turtles often get caught in them.

The manatee, or sea cow, is an underwater grazing mammal. Manatees look almost human when they sit upright in the water. The "mermaids" that sailors used to report seeing might really have been manatees.

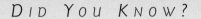

Dugong
The dugong is a relative of the manatee.

Leatherjacket
These get their name from their rough skin.

paddleweed

Fan-mussel
Fan-mussels anchor themselves in the sand.

wireweed

Underwater Meadows

There are places under the sea where grass grows and cows graze—just like on land. Beds of sea grass are tucked away in sandy areas protected from the swells of the open ocean. Sea cows and sea turtles graze in the warm, sheltered waters. Lobsters feed on scraps and hunt for small animals. Sea grass beds are also good hiding places for young fish and prawns.

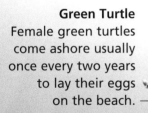

Green Turtle
Female green turtles come ashore usually once every two years to lay their eggs on the beach.

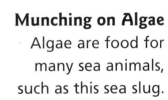

Munching on Algae
Algae are food for many sea animals, such as this sea slug.

Blue Swimmer Crab
These crabs bury themselves in the sand with only their eyes showing.

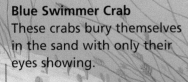

LIVING TOGETHER

Some underwater animals live together and help one another. Clownfish hide from enemies in the stinging tentacles of sea anemones. Remora fish have suckers on their heads that they use to attach themselves to sharks and rays. Remoras eat the parasites that collect on the animal.

Safe Tentacles
A layer of mucus protects clownfish from being stung by the tentacles of sea anemones.

Cleaner Fish
Some fish are helpful cleaners. This little goby is cleaning a grouper by eating the parasites attached to its skin.

Hitching a Ride
Remora fish surf the waves made by swimming rays. They can also attach themselves to get an easier ride.

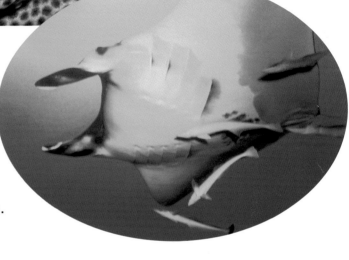

Jellyfish Nursery
Young jacks and driftfish take shelter in the stinging tentacles of jellyfish. Once these fish grow into larger, fast-swimming adults, they no longer need the jellyfish's protection.

FANTASTIC FISH

Sea creatures have developed clever ways of using their bodies to survive in their watery homes. Some fish use their fins as oars to help them swim. Other fish use their fins to hang onto rocks or even to walk! A broken arm is no problem for a sea star. If one of its arms breaks off, it can grow a new one in a few weeks.

Lizard Fish
The lizard fish buries itself in the sand and then darts out to grab its prey.

Splendid Toadfish
The splendid toadfish can walk along the bottom of the ocean using its fins as legs.

Flying Gurnard

The flying gurnard can't fly—but it can walk on the bottom of the ocean. It uses its fins like legs.

Inside a Sea Star

A sea star has lots of little tube feet, each with a tiny sucker. The sea star uses its sucker feet to climb rocks and open shellfish.

CORAL REEFS

A huge variety of fish and other creatures live in the shelter of coral reefs. These reefs are built by tiny animals called polyps. Polyps grow upward, building protective tubes around themselves. Some of their food comes from plant cells living in their body. These living masses of growing polyps are very fragile. They can easily be damaged by human snorkelers and divers.

Types of Coral
There are more than 400 species of coral. One type looks like a brain, so it's called brain coral.

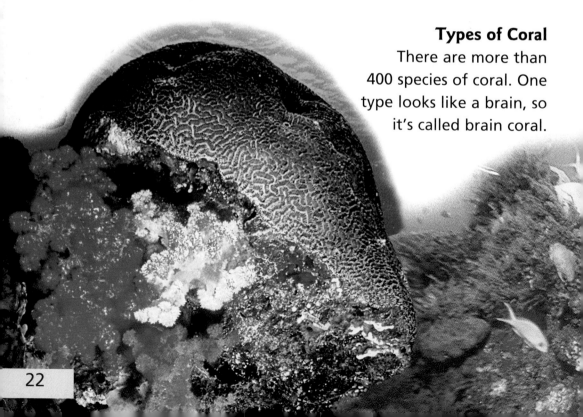

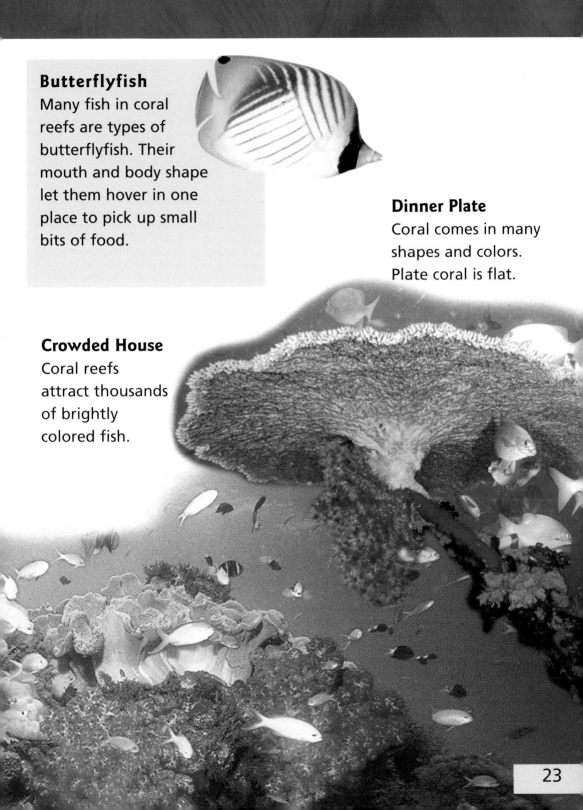

Butterflyfish
Many fish in coral reefs are types of butterflyfish. Their mouth and body shape let them hover in one place to pick up small bits of food.

Dinner Plate
Coral comes in many shapes and colors. Plate coral is flat.

Crowded House
Coral reefs attract thousands of brightly colored fish.

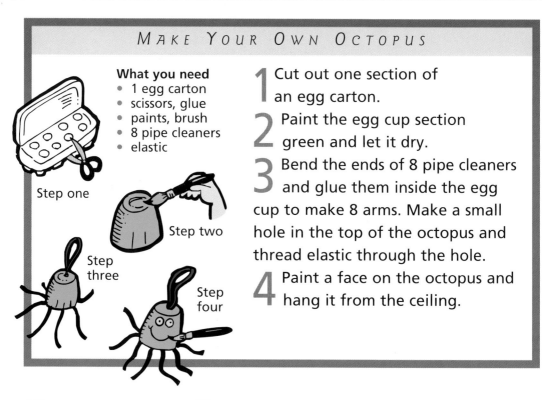

What you need
- 1 egg carton
- scissors, glue
- paints, brush
- 8 pipe cleaners
- elastic

Step one

Step two

Step three

Step four

1 Cut out one section of an egg carton.

2 Paint the egg cup section green and let it dry.

3 Bend the ends of 8 pipe cleaners and glue them inside the egg cup to make 8 arms. Make a small hole in the top of the octopus and thread elastic through the hole.

4 Paint a face on the octopus and hang it from the ceiling.

DANGER BELOW

The oceans are full of beautiful but deadly creatures. Some fish have sharp, poisonous spines on their backs or tails as a defense against enemies. Other sea creatures have stinging tentacles. Many of these creatures live in shallow coastal waters where people wade and swim. People are often stabbed, stung, and bitten—sometimes with fatal results.

Lacy Lion

The lionfish has long, lacy fins. It also has 18 sharp spines, which it uses to inject venom into attackers.

Tiny but Deadly

The blue-ringed octopus is less than 8 inches (20 centimeters) long. Its poison can kill within minutes.

Clear Poison

The jellyfish looks fragile but it has poisonous, stinging tentacles.

How an Estuary Is Formed

Estuaries form in river mouths. Fresh river water flows down and mixes with salty sea water. The sea tides flow in and out of the estuary, changing the level of water.

Mangroves
Mangroves grow in watery mud. Some of their roots develop above the ground.

tributary

mangroves

sea

river

estuary

GATEWAY TO THE SEA

Where fresh river water and salty sea water meet in an estuary, there is always plenty of food. Water birds flock to the mudflats at low tide to feed on tasty worms or scurrying crabs. Sea grasses give shelter to newly hatched fish. Insects, shellfish, fish, and plants share this rich environment. Even people come to fish or collect shellfish and oysters.

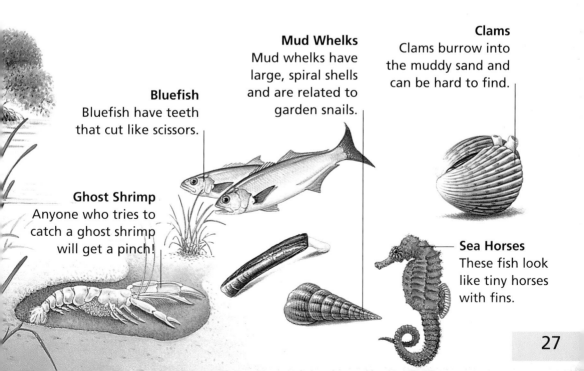

Mud Whelks
Mud whelks have large, spiral shells and are related to garden snails.

Clams
Clams burrow into the muddy sand and can be hard to find.

Bluefish
Bluefish have teeth that cut like scissors.

Ghost Shrimp
Anyone who tries to catch a ghost shrimp will get a pinch!

Sea Horses
These fish look like tiny horses with fins.

Ocean Meets Shore

There are many different shore environments. Some are rocky, some are sandy. In the Galápagos Islands, off Chile, the burning hot rocks and freezing cold sea create a harsh environment. The animals that live there have adapted to life on these strange shores. The Galápagos marine iguana is the world's only seagoing lizard.

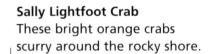

Sally Lightfoot Crab
These bright orange crabs scurry around the rocky shore.

Swimming Lizards
The Galápagos marine iguana can dive to 33 feet (10 meters). It drinks sea water and sneezes the salt out through its nostrils.

Marine Iguana
Sharp claws help them cling to slippery rocks in the surf.

Galápagos Penguin
Penguins fish the waters around the islands.

Flightless Cormorant
The Galápagos cormorant can't fly. It hops into the water to fish, then hops out to dry off.

Galápagos Mockingbird
Mockingbirds use cactus patches as lookouts.

GLOSSARY

archaeologist A person who studies the remains of past human lives and activities.

currents Bodies of water that move continuously in a certain direction.

equator An imaginary line around the world that lies halfway between the North and South Poles.

lava Super-heated, liquid rock that flows up through the Earth's crust and out of volcanic vents.

mammal An animal that grows inside its mother's body before it is born. The young drink their mother's milk.

talons Sharp, curved claws that birds of prey have on their feet.

tentacles Flexible feelers that some animals, such as an octopus, use to feel things and to collect food.

tides The alternating rise and fall of large bodies of water caused by the gravitational pull of the Moon and Sun on the Earth.

tributary A stream that flows into a bigger body of water.

venom Poison that is injected or excreted by certain animals to attack enemies or stun prey, or by plants to trap food.

INDEX

CREDITS AND NOTES

Picture and Illustration Credits

[t=top, b=bottom, l=left, r=right, c=center, F=front, B=back, C=cover, bg=background]

Greg Bridges 8bl. **Jim Chan** 24tl. **Corel Corporation** 13br, 14tl, 16cr, 17br, 18bl, 19bl, 19cr, 19tc, 20cr, 21tl, 22–23b, 23tc, 25tr, 25bc, 28cl, 29tr, 30bl, 4–32 borders, Cbg, FCtl, FClc. **Christer Eriksson** 1c, 2t, 4–5c, 8–9c, 14–15c, 21cr. **Jon Gittoes** 4b, 16–17c, 28–29br. **The Granger Collection** 9tc. **David Kirshner** 20bl, BC. **James McKinnon** 21b. **Colin Newman** 26–27c, 26c. **Trevor Ruth** 6–7c. **Ray Sim** 5tr, 15c. **Mario Sparaciari** 21bc, 25cl, 31tr. **Kevin Stead** 10l, 10–11c, 12–13c, FCbc. **Roger Swainston** 7tr.

Acknowledgements

Weldon Owen would like to thank the following people for their assistance in the production of this book: Jocelyne Best, Peta Gorman, Tracey Jackson, Andrew Kelly, Sarah Mattern, Emily Wood.